ARIANA GRANDE

THE ULTIMATE (UNOFFICIAL) ARIANA GRANDE FAN BOOK 2020

JAMIE ANDERSON

Copyright 2020 by Jamie Anderson, all rights reserved. Copyright and other intellectual property laws protect these materials. Reproduction or retransmission of the materials, in whole or in part, in any manner, without the prior written consent of the copyright holder, is a violation of copyright law.

All images copyright of Ariana Grande.

ISBN-13: 9781701781887
Independently Published

INTRO

Welcome to the Ultimate Ariana Grande Fan Book! One of the hottest and most talented stars in the universe right now, Ariana Grande is just going from strength-to-strength. As we speak she is working hard on her Sweetener tour.

She has come a long way from her time as Cat Valentine on Victorious, hasn't she?! Ari is now one of the most influential and awarded singers out there and we just love her!

So, are you ready to learn more about Ariana and test your knowledge? Let's do this!

— Jamie

CONTENTS

Ariana Grande Quiz 7
    Her early life 8
    Music & Achievements 18
    Her private life 28
    Everything else 34
Ariana Grande Facts 44
Ariana Grande Quotes 52
Ariana Grande Crossword 58

ARIANA GRANDE QUIZ

Here is your chance to test your knowledge of Ariana Grande across four different categories.

Do you know where she was born? What are her parents' names?

Test yourself or test your Ariana loving friends!

Are you ready? Let's go!

ARIANA GRANDE

HER EARLY LIFE

1. Where did Ariana sing the national anthem when she was eight?

. . . . . .

2. What age was Ariana when her parents got divorced?

3. When was Ariana born?

. . . . . .

4. What is Ariana's full name?

. . . . . .

5. Who was Ariana named after?

. . . . . .

6. What was Ariana's first word?

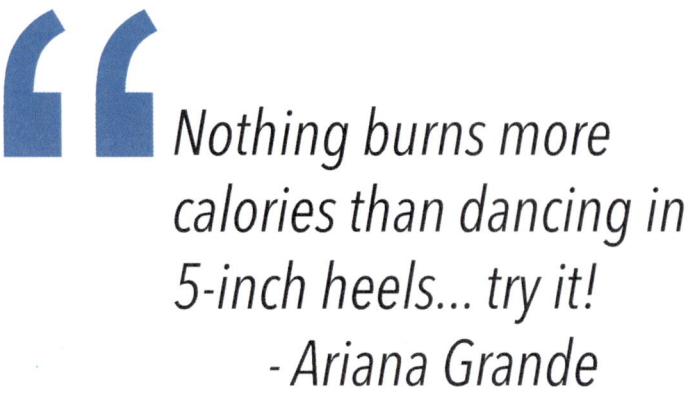
Nothing burns more calories than dancing in 5-inch heels... try it!
- Ariana Grande

7. Where did Ariana make her professional acting debut?

......

8. What are Ariana's parents names?

9. What is Ariana's starsign?

......

10. What did Ariana used to collect?

......

11. What was the first concert Ariana went to?

......

12. When did Ariana first start performing?

13. What schools did Ariana go to?

......

14. What was Ariana's favorite movie when she was very young?

......

15. How many siblings does Ariana have?

......

16. Which celebrity spotted Ariana singing on a cruise ship when she was 8 and said: 'You were meant to do this'?

17. What was Ariana's character's full name in Victorious?

......

18. Finish these lyrics: "She might've let you hold her hand in school, But I'm a show you ___ __ _____

......

19. Where was Ariana born?

......

20. What shoe size is Ariana?

21. How tall is Ariana?

……

22. Does Ariana have a middle name?

……

23. What was the first musical Ariana appeared in at her local Fort Lauderdale Childrens' Theatre?

24. When did Ariana receive her high school diploma?

. . . . . .

25. In what city did Ariana audition for Nickelodeon's Victorious?

ANSWERS

1. AT A HOME GAME FOR THE FLORIDA PANTHERS.
2. AROUND 8 OR 9
3. JUNE 26, 1993
4. ARIANA GRANDE-BUTERA
5. PRINCESS ORIANA FROM FELIX THE CAT
6. "BUBBLE"
7. AS CHARLOTTE ON THE BROADWAY MUSICAL 13, IN 2008.
8. JOAN AND EDWARD
9. CANCER
10. STUFFED ANIMALS, HOCKEY PUCKS AND HALLOWEEN MASKS
11. KATY PERRY IN 2011
12. WHEN SHE WAS EIGHT.

13. PINE CREST SCHOOL AND NORTH BROWARD PREPARATORY SCHOOL
14. THE WIZARD OF OZ
15. SHE HAS ONE HALF BROTHER CALLED FRANKIE
16. GLORIA ESTEFAN
17. CAT VALENTINE
18. HOW TO GRADUATE
19. BOCA RATON, FLORIDA
20. 7.5 US
21. 1.55M (5'0")
22. NO
23. ANNIE
24. 2012
25. NEW YORK

ARIANA GRANDE

HER MUSIC & ACHIEVEMENTS

1. What vocal range does Ariana have?

...... 4 octive

2. What is Ariana's signature stage outfit?

......

3. Name Ariana's five studio albums.

4. What does Ariana call her fans?

. . . . . .

5. When did Ariana put her handprint in cement at Planet Hollywood New York?

. . . . . .

6. What famous festival did Ariana headline in April 2019?

7. How many awards was Ariana nominated for at the 2019 Billboard Music Awards?

. . . . . .

8. How many number one single has Ariana had on the Billboard Hot 100?

. . . . . .

9. How long did it take Ariana to record her first album?

. . . . . .

10. How many singles did Ariana release from her first album?

11. Ariana has a driver's license. True or false?

. . . . . .

12. How many tattoos does Ariana have?

. . . . . .

13. In 2019, Ariana announced that she co-executive produced the soundtrack to which movie?

. . . . . .

14. Which 2017 Disney movie did Ariana record the title song for with John Legend?

15. Who is Ariana's vocal coach?

......

16. How long did it take Ariana's debut album to reach #1 on iTunes?

......

17. How many Nickelodeon Kids' Choice Awards has Ariana won?

......

18. Ariana cried when she met which celebrity for the first time?

19. What Grammy Award did Ariana win in 2019?

......

20. What is Ariana's fourth studio album called?

......

21. Which Whitney Houston song did Ariana perform in front of President Barack Obama and Michelle Obama at the White House?

......

22. In which city did Ariana's *Sweetener* tour start?

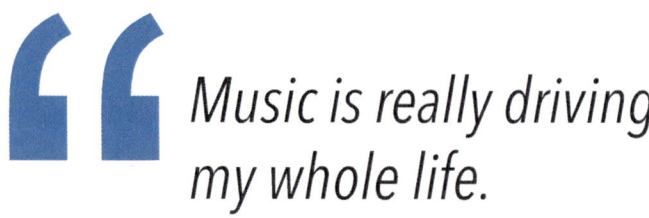

Music is really driving my whole life.

- Ariana Grande

23. Name the three television shows Ariana starred in?

......

24. How many tracks are on her album *Thank U, Next*?

25. What is Ariana's official website URL?

. . . . . .

26. Which magazine named Ariana "Female Artist of the Year" in December 2017?

. . . . . .

27. How many Twitter followers does Ariana have as of October 2019?

. . . . . .

28. Which pop duo did Ariana record the single *Boyfriend* with?

ANSWERS

1. FOUR OCTAVES, SIMILAR TO MARIAH CAREY'S
2. SHORT SKIRTS AND CROP TOPS WITH KNEE-HIGH WHITE BOOTS
3. YOURS TRULY, MY EVERYTHING, DANGEROUS WOMAN, SWEETENER AND THANK U, NEXT
4. "MY LOVES"
5. DECEMBER 22, 2011
6. COACHELLA
7. NINE
8. TWO
9. THREE YEARS
10. FIVE
11. TRUE
12. 44

13. CHARLIE'S ANGELS

14. BEAUTY AND THE BEAST

15. ERIC VETRO. HE IS ALSO KATY PERRY'S VOCAL COACH.

16. 15 MINUTES

17. FIVE

18. JIM CAREY

19. BEST POP VOCAL ALBUM

20. SWEETENER

21. I HAVE NOTHING

22. ALBANY, NEW YORK

23. VICTORIOUS, SAM & CAT, SCREAM QUEENS

24. 12

25. WWW.ARIANAGRANDE.COM

26. BILLBOARD MAGAZINE

27. 66.8 MILLION

28. SOCIAL HOUSE

ARIANA GRANDE

HER PRIVATE LIFE

1. How many pet dogs does Ariana have?

......

2. Can you name all of her dogs?

......

3. How old was Ariana when she had her first kiss?

4. What comedian was Ariana Grande engaged to in 2018?

. . . . . .

5. Why does Ariana always wear her hair in a ponytail?

. . . . . .

6. Who was Ariana's first celebrity crush?

. . . . . .

7. Where does Ariana live?

8. Which fictional character has Ariana said she would marry?

. . . . . .

9. What is Ariana's favorite type of footwear?

. . . . . .

10. What is the name of Ariana's half-brother and best friend?

. . . . . .

11. What type of food does Ariana eat every day?

. . . . . .

12. Ariana and her ex, Big Sean, recorded two songs together. Can you name them?

13. How does she describe her ex, the late Mac Miller, in the track Thank U, Next?

. . . . . .

14. How many fragrances has Ariana released?

ANSWERS

1. NINE
2. COCO, TOULOUSE, CINNAMON, STRAUSS, LAFAYETTE, PIGNOLI, MYRON, SNAPE AND LILY.
3. FOURTEEN
4. PETE DAVIDSON
5. BECAUSE SHE HAS BAD HAIR LOSS FROM DYEING HER HAIR RED EVERY WEEK FOR HER ROLE IN VICTORIOUS.
6. JUSTIN TIMBERLAKE, WHEN SHE WAS THREE.
7. SHE SPENDS MOST HER TIME AT HER HOUSE IN BEVERLEY HILLS.
8. THE COOKIE MONSTER
9. HEELS

10. FRANKIE

11. STRAWBERRIES. SHE EATS AT LEAST FIVE A DAY.

12. 2013'S RIGHT THERE AND 2014'S BEST MISTAKE

13. AS AN 'ANGEL'

14. SEVEN

ARIANA GRANDE

EVERYTHING ELSE

1. What is Ariana's favorite color?

......

2. What is Ariana most afraid of?

......

3. What is Ariana's favorite movie?

4. What is Ariana's favorite board game?

. . . . . .

5. What does Ariana's mom do for a job?

. . . . . .

6. Which TV show did Ariana's brother appear on?

. . . . . .

7. What is Ariana's natural hair color?

. . . . . .

8. On which cheek does Ariana have a dimple?

9. What is Ariana's favorite cereal?

. . . . . .

10. What are Ariana's favorite animals?

. . . . . .

11. Who is Ariana's favorite actress?

. . . . . .

12. What are Ariana's nicknames?

. . . . . .

13. How many views did Ariana's song Thank U, Next have on Youtube in the first 24 hours?

14. What is the name of Ariana's 2019 tour?

. . . . . .

15. Which Ben Stiller movie did Ariana cameo in?

. . . . . .

16. Who are Ariana's main fashion inspirations?

. . . . . .

17. What is Ariana allergic to?

. . . . . .

18. Where does Ariana have a birth mark?

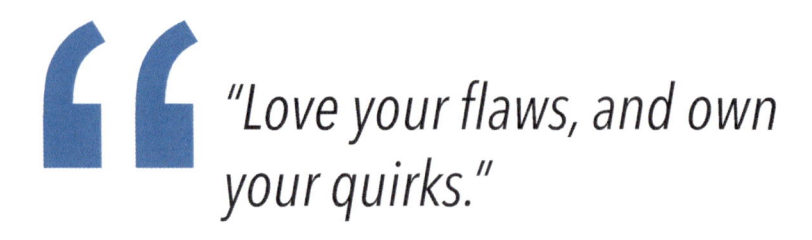

> *"Love your flaws, and own your quirks."*
>
> *- Ariana Grande*

19. What language is Ariana studying?

. . . . . .

20. What is Ariana's favorite ice cream flavor?

21. What does Ariana's dad do for a job?

. . . . . .

22. What was the color of Ariana's dress for her performance at the White House?

. . . . . .

23. How much is Ariana Grande reported to be worth in 2019?

. . . . . .

24. Why did Ariana abandon Catholicism?

25. What car does Ariana drive?

. . . . . .

26. Who were the opening acts of her Sweetener tour at the North American shows?

. . . . . .

27. Which of Ariana's Victorious co-stars made cameos in her Thank U, Next video?

. . . . . .

28. What long-term health problem does Ariana have?

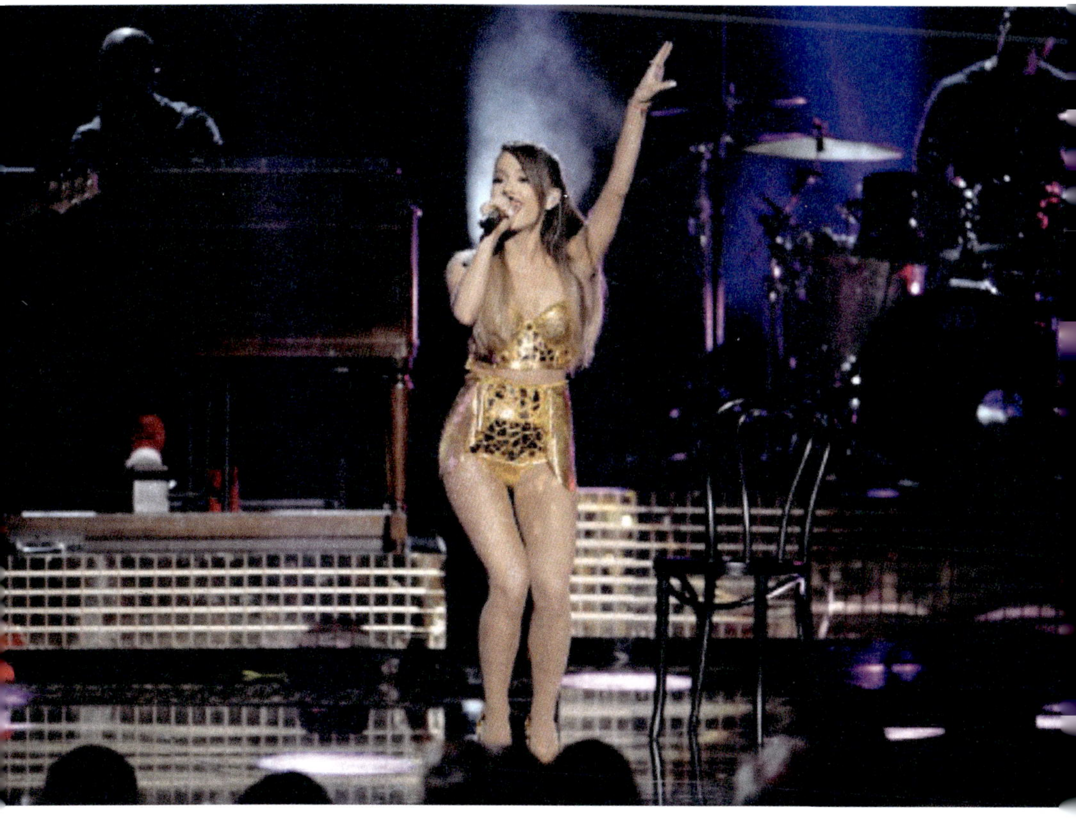

ANSWERS

1. LAVENDER
2. HEIGHTS
3. BRUCE ALMIGHTY
4. MONOPOLY
5. CEO AT A COMMUNICATIONS COMPANY
6. BIG BROTHER 16
7. BROWN
8. THE LEFT CHEEK
9. COCOA PUFFS
10. SEAHORSE
11. JENNIFER GARNER
12. RIRI, ARI AND LITTLE COW
13. OVER 55 MILLION. A RECORD!
14. SWEETENER
15. ZOOLANDER 2

16. MARILYN MONROE AND AUDREY HEPBURN

17. CATS, BANANAS AND DARK CHOCOLATE

18. ON HER LEFT SHOULDER/BACK

19. SPANISH

20. CHOCOLATE

21. HE OWNS A GRAPHIC DESIGN FIRM IN FLORIDA

22. BLACK

23. $50 MILLION

24. IT DOESN'T SUPPORT LGBT RIGHTS

25. A WHITE RANGE ROVER

26. NORMANI AND SOCIAL HOUSE

27. ELIZABETH GILLIES, DANIELLA MONET AND MATT BENNETT

28. SHE IS HYPOGLYCEMIC

ARIANA GRANDE
FACTS

Ariana loves going to the beach in the middle of the night. She finds it calming.

· · · · · ·

Ariana has really bad eyesight and wears contact lenses most of the time.

· · · · · ·

Despite being scared of heights, Ariana loves rollercoasters and theme parks.

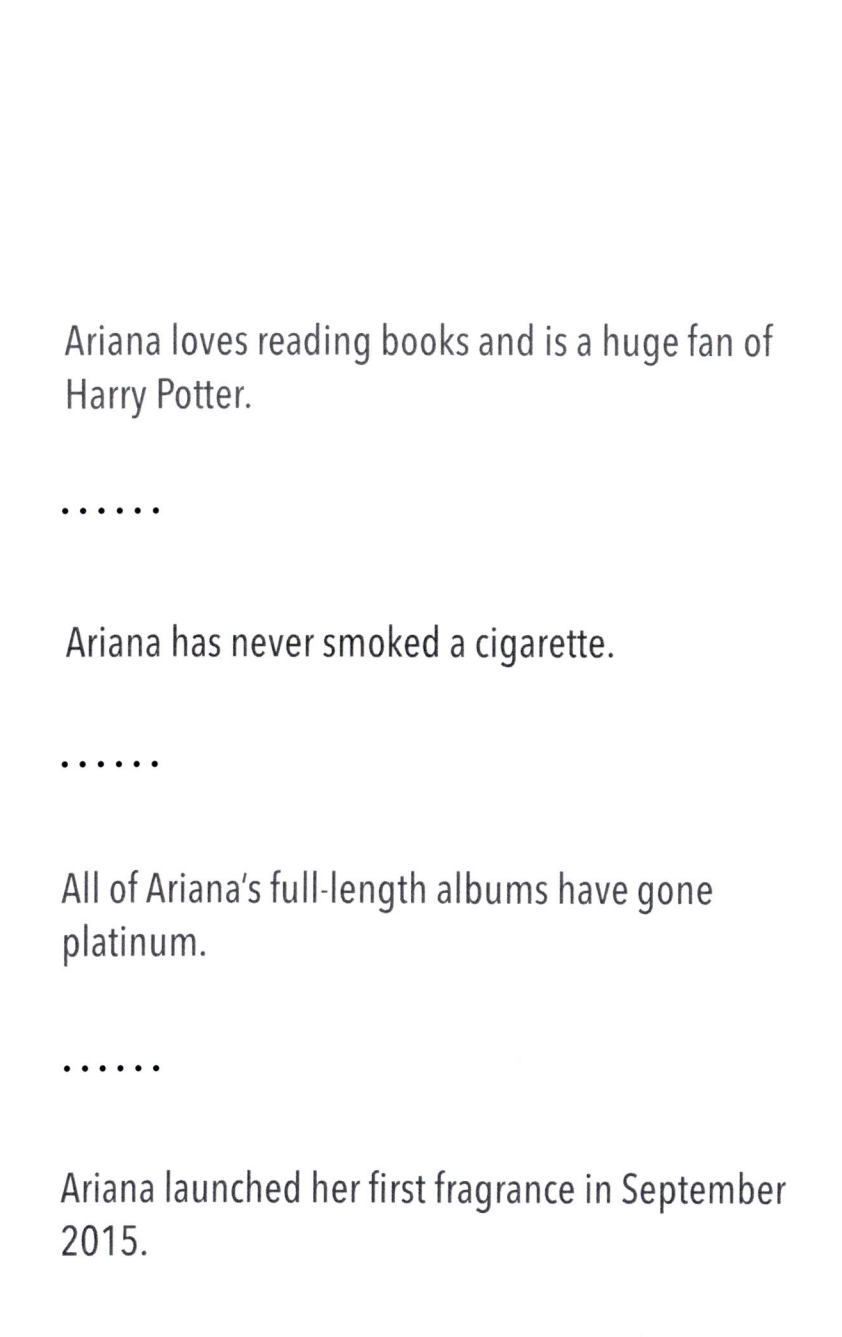

Ariana loves reading books and is a huge fan of Harry Potter.

. . . . . .

Ariana has never smoked a cigarette.

. . . . . .

All of Ariana's full-length albums have gone platinum.

. . . . . .

Ariana launched her first fragrance in September 2015.

Ariana is a native Floridian.

. . . . . .

Ariana loves to sleep in as little clothing as possible. Her grandma taught her this.

. . . . . .

Ariana has a major obsession with horror movies and has done since she was young.

. . . . . .

One of Ariana's best friends, Jennette McCurdy, accidentally made Ariana's phone number public and later apologized.

At the age of ten, Grande co-founded the South Florida youth singing group Kids Who Care, which performed for charitable fundraising events, raising over $500,000 for charities in 2007 alone.

. . . .

Ariana is a vegan, meaning she doesn't eat meat or animal products.

. . . .

Ariana's favorite designer is Chanel.

. . . .

Ariana's favorite subject is science.

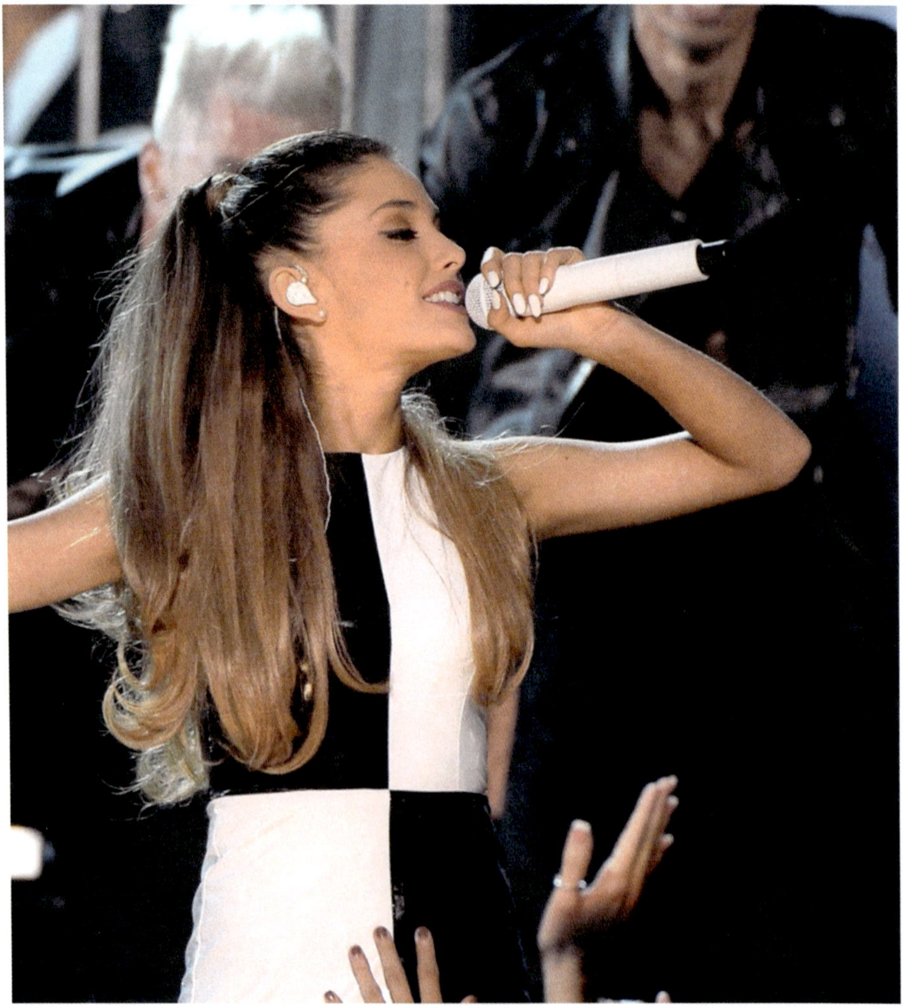

Ariana's song, Baby I, was originally written for Beyonce. Her song Break Free was written for Austin Mahone.

. . . . . .

Ariana is said to be worth over $50 million.

. . . . . .

Ariana's favorite foods are salmon and vegetables.

. . . . . .

Ariana's favorite perfume is Pink Sugar.

. . . . . .

Ariana's favorite television shows are Gossip Girl and Project Runway.

. . . . . .

Ariana used to be a cheerleader.

Ariana's Instagram account has 165 million followers. Her handle is @arianagrande

・・・・・・

When she released Thank U, Next she broke the record for the largest streaming week for a pop album.

・・・・・・

Ariana's mom thought she'd grow up to be a serial killer because she liked wearing Halloween masks.

・・・・・・

Ariana has said that she loves animals more than she loves most people. This is partly why she is a vegan.

・・・・・・

When Ariana is not wearing heels, she walks around on her tippy toes.

Ariana is hypoglycemic, meaning she has low blood sugar.

. . . . . .

At school one time, Ariana filmed her teacher shouting at her.

. . . . . .

Ariana can do an amazing impression of Celine Dion, which she did on Jimmy Fallon.

ARIANA GRANDE
QUOTES

"Everyone is beautiful, everyone is perfect and everyone is lovely."

......

"Be happy with being you. Love your flaws. Own your quirks. And know that you are just as perfect as anyone else, exactly as you are."

"Some people will find any reason to hate. Don't waste your time. Lighten up! It takes so much less energy to smile than to hate. Enjoy life."

. . . . . .

"If anyone tries to bully you don't let them. Take the positive energy form a ball of rainbow power and just, like shove it."

. . . . . .

"Life is beautiful. Be thankful for everything.

"Take a load off, don't take everything so seriously. And just be happier."

· · · · · ·

"If you're passionate about something then it will definitely work out for you. You should never stop believing in something, and you shouldn't listen to anyone who tells you otherwise. Never give up on something you love."

· · · · · ·

"Destroy your ego. Free hugs. Sing your hearts out in the street. Rock 'n roll."

> *Plant love; grow peace.*
> *- Ariana Grande*

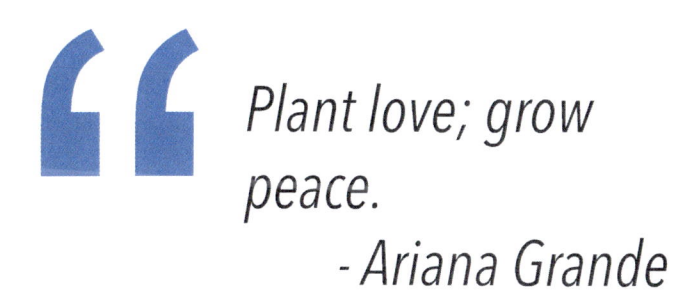

"The best fashion advice I'd say would be just to do what makes you comfortable and what makes you feel cute. And that's how you're gonna look your best. Because when you feel your best, everybody else can feel it too."

"I love my fans so much! I know I say it all the time, but I really appreciate all the things they have done for me."

. . . . . .

"Love is a really scary thing, and you never know what's going to happen. It's one of the most beautiful things in life, but it's one of the most terrifying. It's worth the fear because you have more knowledge, experience, you learn from people, and you have memories."

. . . . . .

"Don't ever doubt yourselves or waste a second of your life. It's too short, and you're too special."

"I love nerdy, cute, quirky boys who don't take themselves too seriously."

. . . . . .

"I'm so thankful for the Internet because actors and singers and performers now have a way to connect with their fans on a very personal level which I think is quite special."

. . . . . .

"One of the most terrible feelings in the world is knowing that someone else doesn't like you. Especially when you don't know what you've done to deserve it."

ARIANA GRANDE
CROSSWORD

W	M	F	E	G	D	S	A	S	T	J	C
E	N	L	D	Q	W	E	F	W	R	H	A
V	B	O	S	J	K	O	J	E	E	S	L
B	A	R	I	A	N	A	G	E	W	P	I
M	T	I	E	C	S	A	D	T	Q	O	F
Y	Y	D	M	U	S	I	C	E	S	N	O
L	U	A	H	D	S	A	X	N	C	Y	R
O	T	H	A	N	K	U	N	E	X	T	N
V	D	D	H	R	T	E	W	R	D	A	I
E	O	G	N	Q	W	E	G	D	A	I	A
S	G	V	F	M	O	N	O	P	O	L	Y
P	S	D	A	N	G	E	R	O	U	S	F

58

Can you find all the words below in the crossword puzzle on the left?

ARIANA ✓
DOGS ✓
FLORIDA ✓
SWEETENER ✓
THANK U NEXT ✓
MUSIC ✓
DANGEROUS ✓
MY LOVES ✓
PONYTAIL
MONOPOLY ✓
CALIFORNIA ✓

How did you go?

Are you a total Ariana Grande fan?! Let us know how you did on the quiz, and tell us some of the most interesting things you learnt about Ari in a review on Amazon.

Do you have more cool facts to share? We'd love to hear from some of our fellow Ariana-lovers, so don't be shy!